LICENSED to S.N.A.P.

Leveraging anger as a powerful tool

Author - Jawann K. Wills, LCSW-C

© 2021 Jawann K. Wills. All rights reserved.
Published by Wills Family Publishing No portion of this book may be reproduced in any form without permission from the publisher, except as permitted by U.S. copyright law.

Year 2021
YOUNIVERSAL GROWTH LLC

ISBN: 978-1-7342496-4-4

TABLE OF CONTENTS

Part 1 - Why so Angry?
Part 2 - Anger is like a Powerful Tool
Part 3 - Anger Essentials
Part 4 - Licensed to S.N.A.P

Why so Angry?

Anger is essential for survival! Anger is as important to the mind, as legs are to the body. Imagine being face to face with danger and not being able to activate your legs! Imagine sweating profusely, looking for help, unable to respond, feeling frozen in time! We're likely to be victimized in that situation.

Many of us believe that people who have "anger" have a problem. That's like saying people who have "legs" have a problem (Haha...a little joke). The truth is, those who cannot think and respond rationally when they begin to feel strong emotions can put themselves and others in harm's way. The solution is learning ways to intentionally use anger as an asset and not a liability. In fact, research suggests "developing specialized techniques to improve thinking and responding can increase the effectiveness of anger management. These techniques reduce anger as well as depression, while improving social skills" (Flanagan, Allen, Henry).

So yes, not being able to manage your anger by thinking rationally can be self-destructive, self-defeating, and can cause unintended harm to others. However, the ability to intentionally use anger in a rational way for self-defense or to combat injustice, is a powerful and useful life skill to develop. I'd like us to refer to this ability as a "License to S.N.A.P."

Anger is like a Powerful Tool

Relax for a second, take a deep breath and calm down. Before we run out, start a fight, and face defeat in the name of "leveraging anger as a powerful tool," let me explain something.

Having anger is like owning a car. We don't drive through an intersection without stopping and paying attention to oncoming traffic. We MUST wait for the right time to make a move.
Before we can become licensed to drive, we need to gain and demonstrate an understanding of the rules of the road, right? Then it would make sense to gain and demonstrate an understanding of the rules of self-control before we can become "Licensed to S.N.A.P."

This guide will provide us with an assessment strategy that can be used to help us assess if an anger fueled response is rational and applicable in an anger provoking situation.

Anger Essentials

There are 3 primary ways for us to respond to feelings of anger. We can choose to suppress our anger, balance our anger, or escalate our anger. When we escalate our anger, we can potentially graduate from anger to rage. Rage is when we relinquish control of our anger. In many cases, escalating our anger results in physical aggression toward others.

There are times when we respond with an anger fueled response and the activating event that led to that decision does not call for such a response. On the contrary, there are also times when we suppress our anger instead of using it to defend ourselves or save our loved ones from physical harm. In these cases an anger fueled response may have been rational.

In reality, it is not uncommon to witness one of us struggling to muster up enough anger to fuel an act of aggression when a situation provokes us to do so. This experience can often lead us to feelings of shame and guilt. So how do we avoid feelings of rage, or shame and guilt? How do we know If we are supposed to respond with physical aggression or not? When is it okay for us to release pent-up rage?

Licensed to S.N.A.P

Many of us are triggered by things that remind us of our insecurities, or that make us feel unsafe. Those triggers can stem from; childhood trauma, to negative statements people have made about us. We can also feel insecure, or triggered from the expectations of others, not being prioritized, or by being lied to by someone we love. While feelings of disappointment, frustration and anger are very rational emotions, none validate a physical assault. So, when is it ok to punch somebody in the face? Well, Rener Gracie, the most famous Brazilian jiu jitsu martial artist said; "every fight you avoid is a fight you win". With that being said, different situations call for different responses.

In this assessment strategy, we use the term "snap" as an acronym (S.N.A.P). It serves as a mental checklist and technique for assessing how rational a rage/anger fueled response is in an anger provoking situation.

Before we become "Licensed to S. N. A. P." we should first assess our safety. Is our safety truly at risk? Why do we believe we are unsafe? What proof do we have? Are we embarrassed because we are the butt of a joke (non-physical threat)? It may be more rational to communicate assertively if we feel embarrassed, then to respond with physical aggression. Are we upset because someone has broken into our home (real physical threat)? In America, some states allow us to defend our home with deadly force, while others require us to exercise a "duty to retreat". Knowing the law is a crucial and a critical component of healthy decision making, and anger management.

Are we at risk of a physical attack? Is someone invading our personal space and threatening to cause us immediate harm (real threat), or are we upset because someone we like wants to spend time with someone else (non-threat)? Disputing evidence we believe we have, and assertive communication are both interventions that often bring about clarity and help to establish boundaries in relationships.

After we assess our safety concerns (S), assess the negative consequences (N) associated with an anger fueled response. What are those consequences? Are the consequences out of proportion with the offense? Is it likely that we will be arrested? If we don't respond with rage, will there be a consequence that is worse than going to jail to us? Seeking mediation, or calling for police assistance in more serious situations can be a healthy way to deal with disputes that may bring negative consequences such as jail time or imprisonment. Some cultures do not support, trust, or feel comfortable involving law enforcement in their disputes. However, taking justice into our own hands can be a life changing decision.

Next, we should assess what it is we are trying to Accomplish (A). Is rage the only way to accomplish that goal? Are we looking to discourage people from making jokes about us (small victory), or are we looking to preserve the safety of our family (large victory)? Would we like to achieve an understanding within a complicated relationship or are we looking to destroy an enemy before they destroy us? Being mindful of our goals and aware of what can be gained and lost in an anger provoking situation can guide us toward the healthiest course of action.

Last but not least, we should assess if a rage response will bring us a sense of Pride (P). Will we feel justified for releasing control of our anger? Will we be excited for the children we care about to copy the same behavior as we did in a similar situation? Will the problem be resolved? Are we leveraging anger as a powerful tool, or are we reacting to an insecurity or trigger? We shouldn't only worry about what others will think about us, but we should consider how we will feel about ourselves when it's over. We are the ones living our experience. Journaling and practicing gratitude (being thankful) can often help us to identify our triggers, prioritize the things that are most important in our lives, and reduce the frequency of being manipulated by pride.

Once we assess the situation (and ourselves) and determine that our safety is not at risk, that the negative consequences are out of proportion with the offense, that our goal is to establish an understanding, and that we would like to be proud of our response in the near and distant future, we may conclude that a rage/anger-fueled response will be inappropriate. As we review and consider the answers to each question in this guide, we may notice that there are few absolutes. The answer to each question depends on our worldview, circumstance, instincts, and what has worked for us in the past (Ellis).

Becoming "Licensed to S. N. A. P. " is about giving ourselves permission to respond appropriately after considering our true intentions and all possible outcomes of a rage/anger fueled response. After developing the skillset to strategically assess anger provoking situations we become "Licensed to S. N. A. P. " The Benefit of the "Licensed to S.N.A.P" assessment strategy is that it challenges us to think about outcomes before choosing a response in an anger provoking situation. When practiced consistently we may become conditioned to think before we respond, limit impulsive reactions and better manage feelings of anger.

References

Ellis, A. J (1995) Rational-Emotive Cognitive-Behavior Therapy 13: 85. https://doi.org/10.1007/BF02354453

Flanagan, R., Allen, K. & Henry, D.J.(2010) J Rational-Emotive Cognitive-Behavior Therapy (2010) 28: 87. https://doi.org/10.1007/s10942-009-0102-4

Guinagh, B. (1987) Catharsis and Cognition. In: Catharsis and Cognition in Psychotherapy. Springer, New York, NY

Tavris, C.(1989) Anger: The Misunderstood Emotion, Simon and Schuster, New York, NY

YOUNIVERSAL GROWTH

Our mission is to teach people the impact that positive thinking, self-reflection, self-respect, and self-care have on our global society. We understand that the way we view the world is not the only way the world is viewed. We envision incorporating best practices from a variety of ideas and systems of belief, which often conflict with one another, into a customized perspective that suits us but does not deny or disregard the views / perspectives of others.

YOUNIVERSAL GROWTH, LLC

www.ingramcontent.com/pod-product-compliance
Lightning Source LLC
Chambersburg PA
CBHW061117070526
44583CB00027B/3324